WHAT IS MONEY?
Why Am I Always BROKE?

William Crumley

OPTION Press

November 2017

WHAT IS MONEY?
Why Am I Always Broke?

INTRODUCTION

I have written two books: <u>Why We Are Always Broke: things we need to know about the economy</u> and <u>Must We Always Remain Broke?</u>

This short essay, <u>WHAT IS MONEY? Why Am I always broke?</u> attempts to highlight some major points of these two books. This book asks certain questions and looks at certain tools falsely presented as answers to these questions.

Why do I always seem to be broke?

Why are so many persons losing their homes and cars?

We hear frequently the Gross National Product is rising - yet I am broke! Who is at fault? Politicians?

Do I simply spend too money?

NONE of these answers seem right!

Maybe we are looking in the wrong place.

May be need to start by asking WHAT IS MONEY? WHERE DOES IT come from? A piece of paper? What makes it valuable?

How is it created? Who creates it?

Money is just a piece of paper. Whether it be a bill or a note which says I have a certain amount of money in my account.

Is money simply a piece of paper which tells me how much money I owe?

Several years ago our paper money was a "Silver Certificate" That means the bill I spend is backed by a certain amount of a precious substance.

Today money says "Federal Reserve Note". With a 20 trillion dollar DEBT the result is $45,000 for each person. Why can't I just walk into a central bank and say "give me my $45.000"? WELL! The note does not tell me how much money the bank owes me BUT how much I owe the bank. Every dollar

I receive or spend is a dollar I OWE to the Federal Reserve Bank.

This may sound strange but every dollar I receive or spend is a note which certifies how much I owe to the Federal Reserve Bank.

A friend bought a home. It has REAL value. He received a piece of paper which has no value.

The paper states that he owes X number of dollars to the Federal Reserve Bank.

If my friend does not "pay" his note, the bank from which he borrowed the money will take his home or whatever he borrowed the money to buy his DEBT. No new money has been created - except the amount my friend already used to pay off his **NOTE**. Even this is simply trading one **NOTE** for another **NOTE**.

What happens to the "money" my friend spent? The bank will take this useless piece of paper (**THE NOTE**) and "sell" it to another bank. The **NOTE** can be "sold" several times. No money is created.

It has simply been passed from one bank account to another. In the process my friend lost his home.

This process of changing notes between individuals has been expanded. Nations pass their notes with one another. This exchange often leads to **WAR**.

The Bank for International Settlements (BIS) was set up after World War 1 to oversee the process of German repayment after World War 1. It is a bank set up under Nazi control. The USA to whom much of the DEBT was owed, put up much of the money to pay off the DEBT.

TALK ABOUT VOODOO ECONOMICS!!! This bank still exists. It does on an international level what USA banks do to my friend (and others) at a local level.

This bank (BIS) is now a combination of the central banks of many nations. These banks control the economy of each member nation. Each year BIS issues a large volume which describes the state of the economy in each Nation. Information in the volume is a major factor determining the financial stability of each nation and what is needed to sustain the economy of that nation. BIS is dominated by a few large nations which control the world's economy.

What BIS does on an international level, the Federal Reserve Bank does on a national level and local banks do locally. In each action of a bank, the "money" exchanged is based on DEBT.

Holiday Inn borrowed a large sum of money. It then used that DEBT as an "investment" to borrow a similar amount of money. This is stated in a proxy statement Holiday Inn issued to the federal government.

Donald Trump attempted to buy out Holiday Inn. It was eventually sold to a British corporation.

A citizen group (OCCUPY MOVEMENT) was organized to call attention and hopefully bring some useful change in the U. S. banking system. OCCUPY was shut down by a Supreme Court order. The movement continued at local levels.

In Ohio a local OCCUPY group filed a legal document stating the bank could not seize any property unless they could provide the original bill of sale. The OhioSupreme Court upheld that claim. The bank had to return the property seizws to its owner.

Banks became greedy and seized many homes. These homes became liabilities.

The banks began to sell the homes for $500 to any chartered organization. One **OCCUPY** group obtained a charter, bought the seized homes and returned them to the owner.

OCCUPY had an effect on some persons working on Wall Street. These persons formed a group who plan to send persons into every state in the USA to encourage residents to take their money out of large multinational banks and place their money in local credit unions.

Credit unions are owned and controlled by the persons who place their money in a local credit union.

PUBLIC CITIZEN was founded by Ralph Nader to help citizens of every state work with members of their state legislature to set up a citizen organization to oversee the work of utility corporations to help ensure more just rates for ordinary citizens. This action was shut down by a ruling of the U.S. Supreme Court.

A group of us realized we could not persuade our state legislature to enact such legislation. We tried to organize groups on a county level.

Electric utility groups at this level are often consumer owned. Owners elect other owners to run the co-op.

One county formed such a group. Six persons were the leaders of their group. All 6 were elected to the board of director of the co-op. I suggested that only three persons be elected. The other three form a group to continue oversight of the co-op. They elected all six. At the next election all six were defeated. Today, the group is listed on the internet as "inactive".

There is a common thread to each action mentioned: **MONEY** and especially who controls money. This control extends far beyond monetary control. It also helps foster war, poverty, and other human problems.

I was a student at the University of Notre Dame. I arguged with my economics professor: "You cannot spend money you don't have and you cannot create something out of nothing."

Several years later a friend said: "If you want to know why something happens, follow the money trail."

This book is based on the remark I made to my economics professor and the comment of my friend. I saw truth In my friend's idea but thought it was too simplistic. I began research to point out how simplistic his statement was. The harder I researched the more

I came to realize his comment had truth beyond my wildest imagination. I found individual directors serving on boards of several corporations.

Bankers served on these same boards. Many boards included directors of foreign corporations and banks.

Governments did not cause economic problems. Government approval and financing made it possible for some distortions.

WHAT IS MONEY looks at economic and political forces that underlie the problems cited in this short summary. The economic forces mentioned above could only have happened without political support.

The Bank for International Settlements was set up by governments to assist in payment of *World War 1* DEBTS. At the end of the war an international group was established to deal with economic problems caused by World War 1.

After World War 2 The Bank for International Settlements was no longer needed. The group planning the future decided BIS was not needed. Political action of a member nation worked to continue the bank.

The Federal Reserve Bank also owed its origin to political forces. A small group of bankers met in a private hidden meeting.

They set up a central bank (the Federal Reserve) so a few bankers would control the economy of the USA.

Their action alone would not have created the Federal Reserve Bank. Congressional action was required to create the bank. There was opposition in the Congress. The bill creating the bank was voted on when many members of Congress had gone home for Christmas.

The Federal Reserve Bank joined the international banking group, the Bank for International Settlements. Both exist because of political action. The Bank for International Settlements was dominated by Nazi interests. It was a tool for moving Nazi gold from Germany to a safer nation.

These 2 banks helped create a worldwide system of false money which spread to local banks.

One source of false money came in the form of stock options. The executives of corporations were given corporation stock in addition to their salary. No money was given. When the value of the stock increased the amount in the executive's bank account increased without any real money being created. The Federal Reserve Bank is another source of false money.

The Bank creates money used for commerce in the USA. No real money is created. Billions (trillions) of dollars appear in bank accounts in the USA. Its "money" is used in the actions of the Bank for International Settlements.

When the war in Iraq was over the finances of Iraq were placed under the control of the Federal Reserve Bank.

Gold is false money. For many years an ounce of gold was worth $35 an ounce. Its value became $700 an ounce – 20 times its previous value. No money was created. Bank accounts boomed.

Ads advising persons to invest $5000 in gold. Corporations invest hundreds of million dollars in gold. Whether gold or dollars is the medium of monetary exchange, poorer persons will always be at a distinct disadvante.

Mortgages are false money. Nothing is added to value of home, car, whatefer is mortgaged. Sometimes the value of what is mortgaged decreases. The interest cost to mortgagee is often more times the amount of the original mortgage. They can be transfered to several financial organizations.

Original items mortgaged are forfeited to the person or group who provided money which began the process. Through all these actions no new money is created. But the amount of "money" in the lender's bank account is greatly increased.

Bankruptcy to all appearances seems to take money out of the economy. No real money (only a series of notes) was a part of the original transaction. With the bankruptcy of a corporation or bank the corporation retains the item mortgaged. The amount remaing is used to pay legal fees, court costs, fines, other expenses resulting from the settlement. There is no new money added, simply credit items passed from one entity to another.

Every monetary transaction) involves the payment of interest. These rates are set by the bank or entity lending the "money". These rates are subject to change within the same transaction. This also is false money. No money is involved in the transaction.

Sub Prime loans are also false money. These loans have lower interest rates and are usually given to persons who cannot afford to pay the regular interest on a note. Often the interest rate increaes with the transaction. In some cases interest on the money is greater than the original loan. The money owed continues to rise even when the "loan" is appearantly being paid off.

Globalization allows corporations to put money and goods in tax free nations. Their "sales" are simply items on a credit account. No new revenues result from these tranactions.

Globalization allows nations to trade freely with one another. This sounds like a marvelous boom to nations economies. Often it means goods are produced in a nation that has lower wages for workers. The nations to which the same goods are sold often experience reduction in the number of workers. False money passes from each nation. Producing nations lose items of greater value than the items they export. The importing nations lose tax and other revenues from those who lost jobs. Profits are reaped by money brokers who arrange the transaction.

Like other examples of false money, bankers and brokers reap profits without investing any money.

Inflation is false money. In theory, inflation results from the normal cost of doing business.

Actually, inflation is the result of more money placed in the economy by the Federal Reserve Bank. As mentioned above, money issued by the Federal Reserve Bank is money government owes to the Federal Reserve Bank.

With rising inflation, government is forced to borrow more money from the Federal Reserve Bank. When there is more **DEBT** the federal government pays to the Federal Reserve Bank, a **DEBT** the government passes on to us. This effect of inflation is never explained to us the victims of inflation.

Deregulation is another tool used to create **DEBT**. It allows corporations to use any of the tools described above. When there is no oversight or control, corporations are free to market their products for any price they wish. Higher prices breed more **DEBT** for the consumer.

Bailuots and other government welfare is needed to allow consumers to pay higher prices for goods. Higher prices can cause less consumer purchases.

A Derivatives are another way to create false money. It is like gambling.

A person speculates stock price will lower, sells stock. Another speculates stock price will rise and buys stock of person who speculatws price would fall. Again there is no creation of money. The outcome is determined by the rise or fall of the stock market which is based on false money. Whatever form of money exchange is used, the system is based on DEBT, underlying force in the creation of false money.

Our so called "free market" economy is relly free. For **NO COST** a corporation uses any tool to create false money.

A tool to counteract economy based on **DEBT** is the use of barter. In its simplest form two persons or groups exchange goods with each other.

Both individuals and corporations use barter as a tool for exchanging goods and services. There are more than 500 groups of individuals who use barter.

One estimate claims there are 450,000 corporations engaged in barter. One example of corpation barter I found is a barter exchange between Pepsico and a Russian corpation. Pepsico gave Russian corporation Pepsi in exchange for Russian vodka which. It more than doubled Russian consumption of Pepsi.

An April 1990 report in the *New York Times* "Pepsi will barter for ships and vodka in deal with Soviets" indicates the ships will be used in the transfer of the two drinks. This barter will enable consumption of each product in both nations to increase.

The article also states the barter agreement will affect the value of the Russian Ruble. Barter can also affect monetary trade.

Several groups e.g. American Barter Exchange and Human Finance Group have been formed to help increase barter. All forms of human exchange can be abused. Native Americans bartered with the English: a gun for twenty deerskins. The deerskin was the Native currency. They provided for basic human needs: food, clothing and shelter. It was also used for barter. Guns allowed Natives to kill more deer. So their currency was destroyed.

SUMMARY

Human transactions require some form of currency. That currency needs to be just for all members of the exchange. It also needs to supply basic human needs. If money is not based on human needs and transacted with some form of equality it is false money.

Much of human need today is built on inequality and the false creation of need. A just solution requires an understanding of what money is and what DEBT is.

WHAT IS MONEY? Why Am I Always Broke? looks at both money and DEBT. The book can be found at CreateSpace William Crumley, WHAT IS MONEY? Why Am I Always Broke?

Books Why We Are Always Broke and Must We Always Remain Broke can also be found at CreateSpace William Crumley with the name of the book.

(un)HAPPY READING! William Crumley (author)

www.ingramcontent.com/pod-product-compliance
Lightning Source LLC
Chambersburg PA
CBHW082125220526
45472CB00009B/2300